Understanding Mon...

Money and Trade

Patrick Catel

Heinemann Library
Chicago, Illinois

www.heinemannraintree.com
Visit our website to find out more information about Heinemann-Raintree books.

To order:
☎ Phone 888-454-2279
💻 Visit www.heinemannraintree.com to browse our catalog and order online.

©2012 Heinemann Library
an imprint of Capstone Global Library, LLC
Chicago, Illinois

Edited by Megan Cotugno
Designed by Ryan Frieson
Original illustrations © Capstone Global Library, Ltd.
Illustrated by Planman Technologies
Maps by The Mapping Specialists
Picture research by Mica Brancic
Originated by Capstone Global Library, Ltd.
Printed and bound in China by Leo Paper Products Ltd.

15 14 13 12 11
10 9 8 7 6 5 4 3 2 1

Library of Congress Cataloging-in-Publication Data

Catel, Patrick.
  Money and trade / Patrick Catel.
    p. cm.—(Understanding money)
  Includes bibliographical references and index.
  ISBN 978-1-4329-4635-7—ISBN 978-1-4329-4642-5 1.
Commerce—Juvenile literature. 2. Free trade—Juvenile literature. 3. International trade—Juvenile literature. 4. Money—Juvenile literature. I.Title.
  HF353.C38 2012
  382—dc22   2010038049

Acknowledgments

The author and publishers are grateful to the following for permission to reproduce copyright material:

Alamy p. 15 (© JG Photography); Corbis pp. 13 (© Bettmann), 33 (© Car Culture), 25 (© Doug Wilson), 6 (© National Geographic Society/Herbert M. Herget), 38 (© Nevada Wier), 35 (© Ryan Pyle), 22 (© Stephanie Maze), 34 (© Tetra Images), 40 (epa/© Dai Kurokawa), 30 (epa/© Laurent Gillieron), 37 (fstop/© Michael Wells), 19 (Redlink/© Uden Graham), 43 (Reuters/© Antony Njuguna), 14 (Reuters/© China Daily), 28, 41 (Reuters/© Denis Balibouse), 27 (Sygma/Jeffrey Markowitz); Getty Images (AFP Photo/Jewel Samad); iStockphoto.com pp. 31 (© Jim Pruitt), 39 (© Mlenny); Photolibrary p. 10 (Comstock); Shutterstock pp. 12 (© ActinicBlue), 8 (© Denis Vrublevski), 23 (© guentermanaus), 7 (© Paul Picone), 26 (© PeJo), 5 (© Russell Shively), 21 (© Sosha).

Cover photograph of a large container ship in a dock at Antwerp Harbor reproduced with permission of Shutterstock (© Anyka).

We would like to thank Michael Miller for his invaluable help in the preparation of this book.

Every effort has been made to contact copyright holders of any material reproduced in this book. Any omissions will be rectified in subsequent printings if notice is given to the publisher.

Contents

You can find the answers to the Solve It! questions on page 45.

Some words are shown in bold, **like this**. You can find out what they mean by looking in the glossary on page 46.

What Is Economics?

Economics is the study of how people use their limited **resources** to meet their needs and wants. To meet these needs and wants, people and companies produce goods and services. Goods are things that are made, sold, and purchased. Services are things that one person pays another person to do. The distribution of these goods and services is made easier through the use of money.

To produce something means to create it. This is called **production**. Goods and services are moved around the world to be sold. This is called **distribution**. When a good or service is finally purchased, it is called **consumption**. The three steps of production, distribution, and consumption make up the economy.

Money

So economics studies the use of money, but what is money? Most people know enough about money to wish they had more of it! People earn money by working. They then use money to buy things they need and want. Money comes in the form of notes (bills), coins, or checks and debit cards. People and businesses put the money they aren't using in a bank to keep it safe.

Money is worth something because the government that makes it guarantees its value. In other words, a dollar is worth a dollar because the government promises it is worth that much. With the guarantee of a strong, stable government, people accept that the dollar is worth a dollar. Money that has the government's backing is called legal tender, and people must accept the money as payment for goods, services, and debts such as car payments. People will trade their goods and services for that **currency**. Currency refers to the type of money that a place uses.

Most countries have their own currencies. The European Union is a group of countries that share a common currency called the euro.

Barter system

Before money, people bartered with one another for goods and services. Barter is another word for trade, but without the use of money. For example, someone might barter, or trade, a chicken with another person in exchange for some clothes. However, that person may not have clothes to trade. In a barter system, each trader has to have something the other wants. It can be difficult and require several trades to finally get what a person needs.

Money makes trade easier

With the invention of money, only two trades were needed. First, people sold something or worked in order to get money. Then they spent that money to buy the things they wanted. People can purchase whatever they need as long as they have enough money. In this way, money has made people's lives easier.

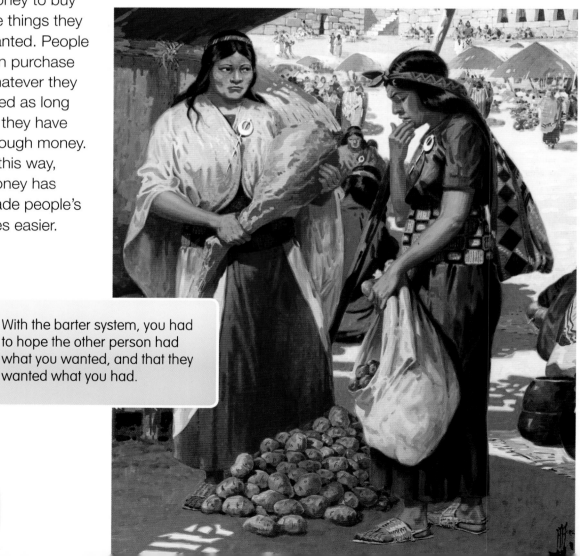

With the barter system, you had to hope the other person had what you wanted, and that they wanted what you had.

The invention of money made trade easier. This silver coin is from ancient Greece.

Gold standard

It took people agreeing on what was valuable for money to work. Gold is a **precious metal**. This means it is rare and everyone recognizes its value. In the past, gold was used as the standard for currency. A standard is something recognized as a point of comparison. So a particular amount of currency was worth a certain amount of gold.

Growth of trade

Money took up less space than goods. This made it easier for people to travel greater distances to trade. In time transportation and technology improved, and the population grew. People began to trade with each other all around the world.

How Did Trade Affect History?

Trade is the activity of buying, selling, and exchanging goods and services. Trade among countries is called international trade. Trade is what allows the stores you shop at to offer many choices of products from all over the world. Without trade, you would have a harder time getting chocolate! Trade has played an important part in human history and exploration.

Exploration

Different countries have different **resources**. Resources are useful things that can be used to increase a country's wealth. This includes natural resources such as minerals like coal and oil, or **precious metals** and stones. It also includes the skills of the country's people and the unique things they make.

Diamonds are rare, precious stones and a valuable resource for countries in which they are found.

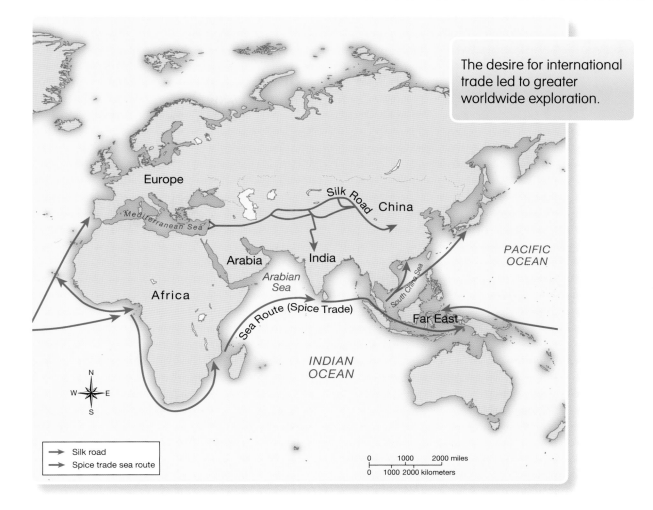

The desire for international trade led to greater worldwide exploration.

The **Silk Road** was first used over 2,000 years ago. It went from eastern China west to the Mediterranean Sea. Silk was a unique product from China. The Chinese guarded the secret to making silk for many years. Chinese traders on the Silk Road exchanged silk for precious metals, glass, wool, and cloth with traders from the Middle East.

Valuable spices such as black pepper and cloves were traded along the Silk Road and other trade routes. Christopher Columbus was trying to find a quicker, easier route by sea to reach the spices of the Far East. Instead he found the West Indies in 1492. Soon, Europeans discovered two whole American continents full of resources. It was not long before they were trading across the Atlantic Ocean for new goods.

Slave women and men on this Georgia plantation were forced to do the hard work of picking cotton.

Colonies

Europeans set up colonies in North and South America. Colonies are settlements in another land that are formed and ruled by the home, or mother, country. Large farms in the colonies called **plantations** grew **cash crops** such as sugar, cotton, and tobacco. These crops were wanted in Europe. However, cash crops required many workers to grow and harvest the crops.

African slaves

Traders brought Africans to work on plantations as slaves. Slaves are people who are owned by other people. They have no rights or freedoms. Slaves working on plantations were poorly treated. They could be punished and killed by their masters.

Triangular trade

The trade that took place between Europe, Africa, and the Americas is called **triangular trade**. The three destination points form a triangle. Traders brought goods such as sugar, tobacco, and cotton to Europe to be sold. They then brought manufactured goods such as guns and metal cookware to Africa to trade for laborers. The traders then packed Africans onto their ships and took them across the Atlantic Ocean to be sold as slaves in North and South America.

The journey of the slave ships became known as the Middle Passage. Many Africans died during the Middle Passage. In the Americas, the Africans were sold into slavery. The traders then loaded their ships with goods once more and headed back to Europe to complete the triangle. By the late 1800s, every country had banned the Atlantic slave trade.

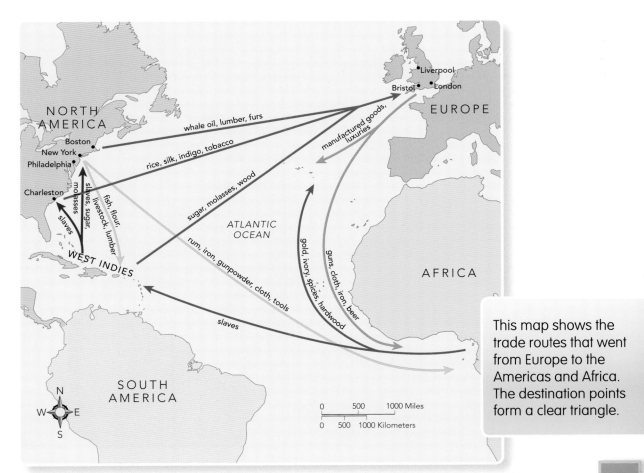

This map shows the trade routes that went from Europe to the Americas and Africa. The destination points form a clear triangle.

How Did Trade Grow?

Eventually colonies of North and South America became new countries, including the United States. These countries continued to trade with other countries. As countries grew and technology improved, international trade became easier. New ideas and machines allowed more goods to be produced cheaply and quickly.

Industrialization

Industrialization refers to the growth of industries that use modern ideas and ways of making things. During the **Industrial Revolution**, there was a change from people producing things by hand to the use of factories and machines to produce more goods for less cost. This happened first in Belgium and Great Britain during the late 1700s, and then in the United States in the mid-1800s.

Factories and smokestacks became common in modern industry.

Assembly lines help produce more goods. The goods are also cheaper to make and cost less to buy.

Mass production

Mass production means making large amounts of goods. It involves the use of designs with interchangeable parts. Interchangeable means the parts are the same for each item being made. People work in an assembly line putting the products together. Each person in the line does a specific part of the assembly process over and over again, rather than putting something completely together.

Division of labor

Division of labor means that the work required to make something is divided into a number of specific tasks. When people have only one task to do, they become very good and fast at that job. This is also called **specialization**, because each worker specializes in one task. More products are produced more quickly, and for less cost.

Improved transportation

An invention called the steam engine helped fuel the Industrial Revolution. Steam engines soon powered ships and locomotives (trains). Before steamships, it took two to three months to sail across the Atlantic Ocean. By steamship the trip was made in about two to three weeks. The steam locomotive made it faster and easier to move people and goods great distances over land.

New technologies, such as airlines, have made international business and trade easier and cheaper.

With steamships and steam trains, more goods were shipped more quickly and at a lower price all around the world. Better engines were invented, and people and goods traveled even faster. The airplane was another amazing new transportation invention. Today, almost any good from around the world can be delivered by air within a day, for a price.

Improved communication

New communication inventions also helped trade. In the past, it took days, weeks, or even months for a written message to arrive, depending on the distance traveled. Today, with telephones, computers, and satellites, people from opposite ends of the world communicate instantly and do business any time day or night.

Solve It!

A company called Old-Timey Shipping can ship 300 sweatshirts to **market** in 8 weeks. A company called New-Fangled Shipping can ship 300 sweatshirts to market in 2 weeks. Assuming a new ship is used each time, how many more sweatshirts arrive at market in 8 weeks using New-Fangled Shipping?

Satellite technology allows people to easily communicate all around the world.

What Does Free Trade Mean?

Free trade is a system where people and businesses can trade goods and services without interference from the government. Under a free trade system, prices of goods and services are determined by **supply and demand**.

Supply and demand

The idea of supply and demand is one of the most important ideas of economics. Supply is how much of something there is available for people to buy. Demand is how much of something people want and can afford to buy.

The demand for something is usually greater when it is brand new.

For instance, an electronics store has 11 copies of a new video game. That is the supply. There are 15 people who want to buy the new video game. That is the demand. Four people are not going to be able to buy the game, because the demand is greater than the supply. Supply and demand are directly linked in a free-trade system. The goal is to have an equal amount of supply and demand in order to have an economy that runs smoothly.

Price

Price is directly related to supply and demand. Usually, the price of something will go up if the demand for that good or service goes up. This is because if a lot of people want something (demand), but there is only a limited number (supply), people who really want it badly will pay more to get it. In other words, the demand goes up, so the price goes up. If the demand goes down, the price will go down.

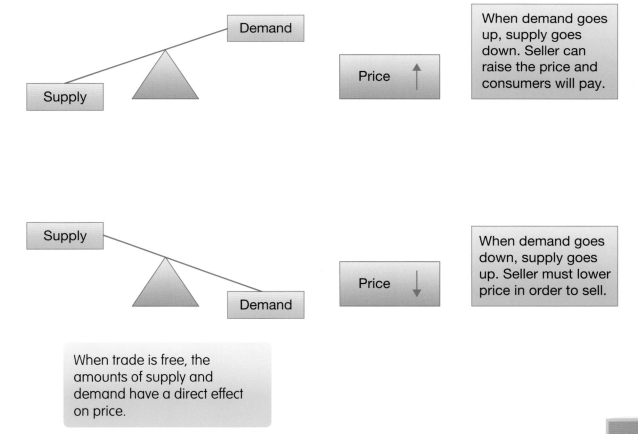

Demand

Supply

Price ↑

When demand goes up, supply goes down. Seller can raise the price and consumers will pay.

Supply

Demand

Price ↓

When demand goes down, supply goes up. Seller must lower price in order to sell.

When trade is free, the amounts of supply and demand have a direct effect on price.

Imports and exports

Imports and **exports** are what make up international trade. Imports are goods produced elsewhere and brought into a country for sale. Exports are goods produced and shipped out of a country for sale elsewhere. So one country's imports are another country's exports, and vice versa.

If a country has more of something than it needs, it might export that good to be sold in a different country. Likewise, if a country needs something it does not have enough of or cannot make, it might import that good. In this way countries help each other meet the needs of supply and demand through trade.

Resources

Countries have different **resources** and amounts of resources. For instance, the United States and Argentina have a lot of farmland and grow a lot of corn. Japan and South Korea have a limited amount of farmland. The United States and Argentina export corn to Japan and South Korea, which means Japan and South Korea import the corn.

Balance of trade

Balance of trade is the difference between the value of exports and imports in a country's economy. A country that exports more than it imports has a trade surplus. A country that imports more than it exports has a trade deficit.

China

The People's Republic of China is the world's second largest trading power. It does over $2.1 trillion of trade a year in combined imports and exports. It also has the greatest trade surplus in the world. This means it exports more than it imports.

GDP

A country's **GDP** is the measure most used to tell the strength of its economy. GDP stands for **gross domestic product**. The GDP is the total value of all goods and services produced within a country during a certain amount of time—usually a year.

In recent years, the United States, Japan, and the People's Republic of China have had the largest GDPs in the world. They are recognized as the world's greatest economic powers. India and Brazil are growing economic powers, because their GDPs are rapidly increasing each year.

World GDP by Sector, 2009

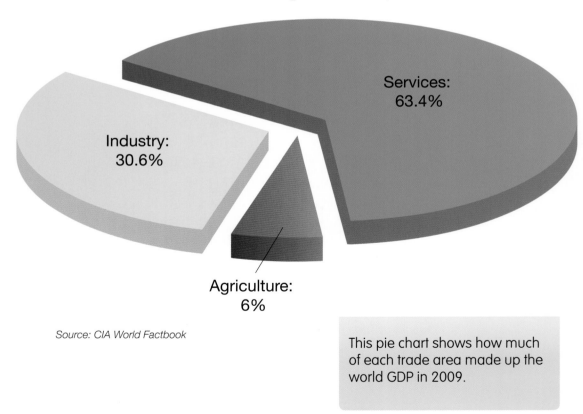

Services: 63.4%

Industry: 30.6%

Agriculture: 6%

Source: CIA World Factbook

This pie chart shows how much of each trade area made up the world GDP in 2009.

Protectionism

Not all trade is free trade. Sometimes a country worries that its economy will suffer if its people buy cheap imports, rather than spend more on similar goods made within the country. To protect its own economy, a country sometimes puts a tax on imports to raise their prices. A tax placed on imported goods is called a **tariff**. The policy of a country interfering with free trade in this way to protect itself is called **protectionism**.

Solve It!

Suppose a pair of shoes you want costs $45. An identical, imported pair costs $40, but has a tariff of 20 percent. With the tariff, the imported pair costs $48, which is $3 more ($48 − $45 = $3). Which pair would you buy? What do you think the country exporting the $48 pair of shoes will do if the shoes don't sell and it loses money?

What Are Trade Agreements?

Sometimes when countries use **protectionism**, other countries react by also placing **tariffs** on **imports**. This can lead to disagreements called **trade wars**. Countries make agreements with each other called **trade agreements** to end trade wars and reestablish **free trade**.

Trade wars

A trade war begins when Country A places a tariff on goods coming from Country B. Country B loses money because of the tariff, and it responds by placing its own tariff on goods coming from Country A. Both countries usually suffer in a trade war, but poor countries are more likely to suffer than rich ones.

These bales of cotton will be loaded onto ships for trade. Countries have often placed tariffs on imported cotton to protect their own cotton industry.

Banana Trade War

United States fruit companies grow bananas on farms in Latin America and sell them around the world, including in Europe. The European Union (EU) is a group of countries that trade as one country (see page 26). In 1993, the European Union raised tariffs on bananas imported from American companies. In response, the United States raised tariffs on goods imported from the EU. Both sides continued to raise tariffs on more goods in the trade war.

Finally both sides took the disagreement to the **World Trade Organization (WTO)**. The World Trade Organization helps nations solve trade disputes and form new trade agreements. After years and many meetings, both the United States and the EU agreed in 2001 to lower their tariffs and end the trade war.

International trade groups

Several international trade groups exist today. These groups help their members by creating trade policies and settling trade disagreements. The World Trade Organization (WTO) is the largest international trade group with over 150 member nations. It was formed in 1995 with the goal of encouraging free trade and setting international trade rules. The WTO has its headquarters in Geneva, Switzerland.

The two largest regional trade groups are the European Union (EU) and the **North American Free Trade Agreement (NAFTA)**. Other regional trade groups include the Association of Southeast Asian Nations (ASEAN) and Mercosur (Southern Common Market) (see page 27).

OPEC

OPEC stands for the Organization of Petroleum Exporting Countries. (Petroleum is another name for oil.) OPEC includes 12 countries that produce and **export** oil. Together OPEC nations hold about 80 percent of the world's oil reserves and produce about 40 percent of the world's oil. This gives them a great amount of influence over the oil **market**.

The 1973 Yom Kippur War was between Egypt, Syria, and its Arab **allies** on one side, and Israel on the other. The Arab members of OPEC threatened an oil **embargo** for any country that supported Israel in the war. An embargo is an official stopping of trade with another country. The United States and other countries that supported Israel suffered from a lack of supply of oil during the 1973 oil crisis.

Due to limited supply
SORRY...
NO
GASOLINE
TODAY

During the 1973 oil crisis, U.S. demand for oil was greater than the supply, and oil and gas prices went up.

European Union (EU)

The European Union (EU) is an economic and political union of countries mostly located in Europe. The European Union formed in 1992 with 12 countries as members. Today it includes 27 countries—16 of which use a common **currency** called the euro.

The European Union is considered as one country when it comes to world business and economics. The **gross domestic product (GDP)** of the European Union, with its member countries added together, makes it one of the two largest economies in the world.

Solve It!

Germany contributes about 20 percent of the European Union's GDP, France about 15 percent, and the United Kingdom about another 15 percent. When added together, what percentage of the European Union's GDP do these three countries contribute? What total percentage do the other 24 EU member countries contribute?

Hint: There can only be 100 percent total.

Sixteen member states of the European Union (EU) use the euro as their currency.

In 1993, President Bill Clinton continued what President George H. W. Bush started and committed the United States to NAFTA.

North American Free Trade Agreement (NAFTA)

The North American Free Trade Agreement (NAFTA) created a trade group including Mexico, the United States, and Canada. It removed most trade barriers (such as high tariffs) among the three countries. The combined GDP of the countries of NAFTA make this trade group the other of the two largest economies in the world (with the EU).

Other trade groups

The Association of Southeast Asian Nations (ASEAN) is a regional trade group of ten countries located in Southeast Asia. Mercosur (Southern Common Market) is a trade group of countries in South and Central America.

Who Makes Sure Trade Is Fair?

Free trade and **trade agreements** work only if all the countries involved agree to follow certain rules. They must also be willing to let a governing body enforce the rules. Only then do trade agreements bring the full benefits of free trade to all of the member countries and citizens.

World Trade Organization

The **World Trade Organization (WTO)** works to build a fair international trading system that runs smoothly. The organization includes over 150 member countries. Together they make up over 96 percent of all world trade. All WTO members make decisions for the group at the Ministerial Conference, which meets roughly every two years.

Member governments must give the WTO their support in order for it to work. Countries often try to bend or break the rules for their own economic benefit. However, the WTO offers the chance for governments to negotiate and solve trade disputes (arguments) rather than allow problems to escalate into armed conflict. In this way, the WTO helps maintain peace as well as orderly trade.

The WTO has helped govern international trade since 1995.

Principles of the WTO

The WTO has certain principles, or ideas, that its members agree to follow. All WTO nations are supposed to be equal and treat each other as equals. They all agree to fair trade and competition, and to try to open their **markets** even further. The WTO also recognizes the need to help poorer countries. It tries to do this by helping poor countries challenge stronger ones in cases where the poor countries are being treated unfairly.

Country GDPs and Populations		
Country	GDP ($ Millions)	Population
European Union	$14,510,000	492,387,344
United States	$14,260,000	310,232,863
China	$8,789,000	1,330,141,295
Japan	$4,137,000	126,804,433
India	$3,560,000	1,173,108,018
Germany	$2,811,000	82,282,988
United Kingdom	$2,149,000	61,284,806
Brazil	$2,025,000	201,103,330
Mexico	$1,482,000	112,468,855
Canada	$1,285,000	33,759,742
Indonesia	$969,200	242,968,342
Turkey	$863,300	77,804,122
Australia	$824,300	21,515,754
South Africa	$495,100	49,109,107
New Zealand	$114,900	4,252,277

This table lists the population and GDP of several countries.

WTO Protests

Many people criticize the WTO. They believe it favors rich countries at the expense of the poor. They also believe the WTO is not concerned enough with protecting the environment or people's rights and health.

Greater freedom of trade helped millions of people around the world break out of poverty (the state of being poor). However, the difference in the **standard of living** between the people in rich and poor countries is more than twice what it was 50 years ago. The difference between how much money rich and poor countries make also appears to be increasing.

For these reasons, thousands of people showed up in Seattle, Washington, in 1999 to protest (speak out against) the Third Ministerial Conference of the World Trade Organization. The protests briefly shut down the WTO meetings. Protests are now common at WTO conferences. There were again clashes between police and protestors at the Ministerial Conference in Geneva, Switzerland, in 2009.

World Bank and IMF

The World Bank is owned by 187 countries, which pay membership dues (money to belong). The World Bank's mission is to reduce worldwide poverty. It provides loans to poorer countries to use for their economic improvement. The International Monetary Fund (IMF) is another organization of 187 countries. The IMF promotes greater worldwide economic cooperation. It also promotes high employment, economic growth, and the reduction of poverty around the world. Like the WTO, some people criticize the World Bank and the IMF.

The headquarters for the World Bank is located in Washington, D.C.

How Do Businesses Benefit from Trade?

The goal of a business is usually to make money. A business does this by selling goods or services for a **profit**. Profit is the money a business gains after its costs are paid. So, profit is affected by how much a business sells, but a business is also affected by how much it spends to do what it does.

A business can increase its profit by selling more, raising its prices, or reducing its costs. Businesses benefit from trade because they have access to more people who will buy their goods. This means they sell more and make more money. Businesses also benefit from trade when it helps them reduce their costs. The costs of doing business include money spent on materials, worker **wages**, energy, and transportation.

Corporations

A **corporation** is a large business organization given legal rights by a state and seen as separate from its owners. Corporations have most of the same rights and responsibilities as an individual. **Shareholders** are people who own parts, or shares, of a corporation. Shareholders benefit from the profits of a corporation. However, since a corporation is seen as separate from its owners, shareholders have some personal protection if a corporation has large debt or goes out of business.

Multinational corporations

A **multinational corporation** is one that operates in more than one country at a time ("multi" means more than one). Some large multinational corporations have **GDPs** greater than some countries! For instance, the GDPs of Wal-Mart and Exxon Mobil are bigger than Pakistan, Venezuela, and New Zealand.

By manufacturing cars in places where resources and labor are cheaper, companies keep costs and prices down. The companies then ship the finished cars to markets around the world.

Exchange rates

The **exchange rate** is the value of one **currency** compared to another. For instance, a British pound might be worth $1.60. Exchange rates of currencies are determined in the **foreign exchange market**, where currencies of different countries are bought and sold. The rates of exchange are constantly changing, even by the minute, based on **supply and demand**.

As an example, in order to buy European goods, you need euros. If a lot of people seek out euros to buy European goods, that means the demand goes up. As we've seen, when the demand goes up, the price also goes up. So an increased demand for the euro means the value of the euro will also increase.

Businesses and consumers from a particular place benefit from a foreign exchange when the currency they are using can buy more of a different currency.

Corporations take advantage of exchange rates by hiring workers in a place where the dollar is worth more by comparison. The corporation pays less in wages for workers, which means its costs go down. When its costs go down, a corporation's profits go up. However, jobs gained in one country may be jobs lost in another.

Solve It!

Suppose the exchange rate of British pounds to United States dollars is £1 = $1.50. You have $30 in your pocket. If you exchanged your $30 for British pounds, how much would you have? If you had £30 instead and exchanged it for dollars, how much would you have?

Cutting costs

Multinational corporations take advantage of exchange rates in order to make more money. For instance, an American or European company might set up a factory in another country where the dollar or euro can buy more of the local currency because of the exchange rate. This means the company will pay less money for **production** and wages, and will therefore have higher profits. By producing goods worldwide, multinational corporations also save on shipping costs and the time it takes for products to reach markets. More products are produced more quickly, for less cost, and are more quickly and easily sold around the world.

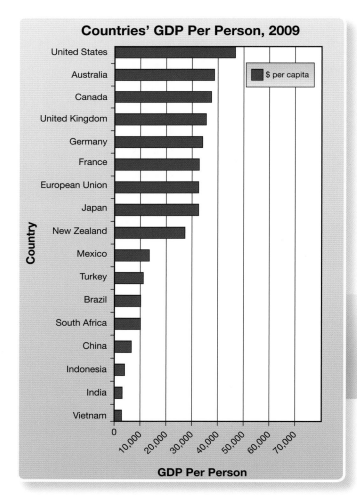

Countries' GDP Per Person, 2009

■ $ per capita

Country (vertical axis)

United States
Australia
Canada
United Kingdom
Germany
France
European Union
Japan
New Zealand
Mexico
Turkey
Brazil
South Africa
China
Indonesia
India
Vietnam

0, 10,000, 20,000, 30,000, 40,000, 50,000, 60,000, 70,000

GDP Per Person

The GDP per person (per capita GDP) gives some idea of how well the country's people are living.

Source: CIA World Factbook

Solve It!

A local electronics company produces flat-panel televisions. The TVs cost $1,200 each to purchase in stores, and the company pays $900 to make each TV. So the company makes $300 profit on each TV sold.

A multinational corporation produces a similar flat-panel television in a factory in a different country. Its TVs also cost $1,200 each to purchase. However, the corporation only pays $700 to produce each TV because it benefits from the exchange rate, lowering its costs. That means the multinational corporation makes $500 profit on each TV sold.

How much more money does the multinational corporation make with each TV sale?

If you could be a shareholder of either company and benefit from its profits, which one would you choose?

Huge cargo ships like this carry millions of tons of goods to be traded all around the world.

What Does Globalization Mean?

Globalization refers to the process by which different societies and regions have become combined in their economies and cultures through international trade. Globalization means that with modern technology and transportation, the world's economies are becoming a single, giant, international **market**. The **WTO** has helped bring about globalization—its members agree to the same rules and ideas and already make up most of the world's trade (96 percent).

This has led to more **free trade** and a high **standard of living** for millions of people around the world. However, it has also had negative effects on certain regions. Many people say that with globalization wealthy nations and **corporations** benefit, while poorer countries and the environment suffer.

This Indian call center for an American business takes advantage of labor costing less in India than in the United States.

Billions of dollars worth of trade take place every day in financial centers of cities like New York City, pictured here.

Criticisms of globalization

One criticism of globalization is that wealthy corporations and countries have the power to drive local producers and sellers out of a market. Since **multinational corporations** are able to benefit from operating and trading internationally, local businesses are sometimes not able to compete.

Critics of globalization say the death of local businesses reduces competition and consumer choice. It also takes some **profits** out of that country's economy, since they go to a foreign corporation. Critics say multinational corporations fight to keep **wages** low. They also say multinational corporations fight against the **regulation** of health, safety, and effects on the environment—especially in poorer, less powerful countries.

Environmental Impact

Increased international trade causes rapid changes to the environment. As globalization continues, trade and environmental concerns seem more and more linked. The WTO has been active in making sure the environment is considered with **trade agreements**. There is an entire committee of the WTO that is devoted to dealing with environmental issues in trade.

One idea is to add environmental costs to products, like a tax. This means businesses would no longer save money by using processes that are cheaper but harm the environment. However, it is difficult to put a value on environmental costs.

Support for globalization

Economists are people who study the way in which money, business, and trade operate. Many economists point out the good of globalization. They say many countries benefit when multinational corporations do business there. Foreign companies often pay employees more than domestic ones. (Domestic refers to something happening within a home country, and not involving other, foreign countries.) Foreign companies often create jobs faster than domestic companies as well.

Supporters of globalization claim it has brought cheaper **imports**, new technologies, and greater market competition to more places around the world. They argue that faster worldwide economic growth will lead to greater wealth and happiness for all people. They say this will then lead to improved working conditions and a cleaner, healthier environment all around the world.

Only time will tell if globalization is an overall positive or negative thing for the world's people.

As long as the world is unequal, people will continue to speak out against globalization.

IN FOCUS:
How Do Pirates Affect Trade?

Pirates have roamed the seas threatening trade ships since ancient times. You may picture the famous pirates who sailed the Caribbean Sea in the 1600s and 1700s, but piracy is not only a thing of the past. Piracy is still a worldwide problem. In fact, piracy is growing more common in parts of the world, and the number of pirate attacks has risen in recent years. In 2009 pirate attacks more than doubled from the year before.

Pirate Activity

Pirates are especially active in certain spots. One is the ocean water between Indonesia and Malaysia. There are also pirate attacks in the Caribbean Sea. The west coast of Africa and the Bay of Bengal in India also suffer from pirate activity. Pirates target waterways with the most trade traffic, since they're usually looking for cargo ships transporting goods. Pirates steal a ship's cargo, but they also often hold its crew for ransom.

Attack on the *Maersk Alabama*

A pirate attack off the east coast of Africa made international news in April 2009. Pirates from Somalia attacked the *Maersk Alabama* on April 8, 2009. The crew fought back and captured the pirate leader for a time. However, eventually he escaped with the other pirates aboard a covered lifeboat. The pirates took Captain Richard Phillips **hostage**. A few days later, on April 12, Captain Phillips was saved by United States Navy Seals in a dramatic rescue.

The attack on the *Maersk Alabama* was the first pirate takeover of a ship flying the U.S. flag since the early 1800s.

Summary

Before money, people traded goods to get what they wanted. The invention of money made trade easier. The desire for trade led to greater exploration of the world. As technology improved and the world's population grew, international trade also grew.

Industrialization and its ideas of **mass production** and **division of labor** (or **specialization**) brought economic growth and a better way of life to many people. Improvements in transportation and communication led to further trade and economic growth worldwide.

Free trade means people and businesses can trade goods and services without interference from government. In a free trade system, prices of goods and services are determined by **supply and demand**.

Imports and **exports** are what make up international trade. **Balance of trade** is the difference between the value of exports and imports in a country's economy.

The policy of a country interfering with free trade to protect itself is called **protectionism**. Protectionism can lead to disagreements called **trade wars**. Countries make **trade agreements** with each other to end trade wars and reestablish **free trade**.

International trade groups such as the **World Trade Organization (WTO)** encourage **free trade**, create international trade rules, and help settle trade disagreements. Regional trade groups such as the EU and **NAFTA** work to help their member countries in ways similar to the WTO.

Globalization refers to the process by which different societies and regions have become integrated, or combined, in their economies and cultures through international trade. Globalization has led to more free trade and a high **standard of living** for millions of people. However, some say that globalization benefits wealthy nations and **corporations**, while poorer countries and the environment suffer. The debate about globalization continues.

Answers to Solve It!

Page 15

Answer: 900

Show Your Work: Old-Timey ships 300 in the 8 weeks, and New-Fangled ships 1,200 in the 8 weeks (8 ÷ 2 = 4) & (300 x 4 = 1,200). The difference is 900 (1,200 – 300 = 900).

Page 21

Answer: You'd probably buy the $45 pair of shoes, since they're the same and you'll save $3. If the exporting country loses money, it may start a trade war by adding a tariff to imports from the country that taxed its shoes. Or it may choose to do more business with a different country instead.

Page 26

First Answer: 50 percent

Show Your Work: 20 percent Germany + 15 percent France + 15 percent United Kingdom = 50 percent total

Second Answer: 50 percent

Show Your Work: Since the total contributions must equal 100 percent, that means the remaining 24 member countries contribute the other 50 percent of the European Union's GDP (100 percent – 50 percent = 50 percent).

Page 35

First Answer: £20 British

Show Your Work: Since each pound is worth $1.50, finding how many times 1.5 goes into 30 will give you the amount of pounds you can get if you exchange your currency (30 ÷ 1.50 = 20).

Second Answer: $45

Show Your Work: (30 x $1.50 = $45)

Page 37

First Answer: The multinational corporation makes $200 more on each TV sold.

Show Your Work: ($500 – $300 = $200)

Second Answer: The multinational corporation makes a higher profit. That means you'd make more as a shareholder of the multinational corporation than you would as a shareholder of the local company.

Glossary

ally (plural is **allies**) country that agrees to help or support another country

balance of trade difference between the value of exports and imports in a country's economy

cash crop crop that is grown to be sold and requires many people to farm

consumption act of purchasing goods and services; people who purchase goods and services are called consumers

corporation big company or group of companies acting together as an organization

currency system or type of money a country uses

distribution the act of moving goods and services around the world to be sold

division of labor process of making goods in which workers are assigned very specific tasks in order to increase the speed and amount of production

embargo official order to stop trade with another country

exchange rate value of the money of one country compared to the money of another country

export something sent to another country to be sold

there; or the act of doing this

foreign exchange market where currencies (money) from different countries are bought and sold, which determines the exchange rates

free trade situation in which goods coming into or going out of a country are not taxed and people and businesses can trade without government interference

globalization process by which different societies and regions have become combined in their economies and cultures through international trade

gross domestic product (GDP) total value of goods and services produced in a country in one year

hostage someone kept as a prisoner by an enemy so that the other side will do what the enemy demands

import something brought from one country into another to be sold there; or the act of doing this

Industrial Revolution period of economic growth in the 1700s and 1800s when industries began to use modern ideas and ways of making things, including factories and machines

market place where goods are sold; buying and selling of goods and services

mass production when products are made in large numbers using machines so that they can be sold more cheaply

multinational corporation large company that operates in more than one country at a time

North American Free Trade Agreement (NAFTA) regional trade group including Canada, the United States, and Mexico

plantation large farm where cash crops are grown

precious metal rare and valuable metal such as gold or silver

production act of producing, or creating, something

profit money gained by selling things or doing business, after costs have been paid

protectionism when a government tries to help industries in its own country by taxing or holding back foreign goods

regulation control over something using official rules

resource something that can be used to increase the wealth of a country or business, such as valuable land or minerals

shareholder person who owns a part, or share, of a business

Silk Road ancient trade route along which silk and other goods were carried west from China and the Far East to the Mediterranean Sea and Europe

specialization idea of the Industrial Revolution where each worker focuses on a single task in order to become an expert at it

standard of living amount of wealth and comfort people have

supply and demand relationship between the amount of goods for sale and the amount of goods people want to buy, and the way that relationship affects prices

tariff tax on goods coming into a country

trade agreement agreement made between countries to establish free trade and end trade wars

trade war situation where nations attempt to damage each other's trade through restrictions and taxes on goods

triangular trade trade among three points that forms a triangle, where one point supplies what the next one wants

wages money paid to workers; money earned by workers

World Trade Organization (WTO) international organization that encourages free trade and sets international trade rules for its members

Find Out More

Books

Andrews, Carolyn. *What Is Trade?* (Economics in Action). New York: Crabtree, 2008.

Bowden, Rob. *Trade*. (The Global Village). Mankato, MN: Smart Apple Media, 2008.

Orr, Tamra. *A Kid's Guide to the Economy* (Robbie Readers). Hockessin, DE: Mitchell Lane, 2009.

Websites

www.kids.gov
Explore and find links to government and money websites.

http://www.pbs.org/wgbh/nova/moolah/history.html
Read about the world history of money and trade.

http://www.usmint.gov/kids/campCoin/timeline/
Learn about money highlights in United States history.

Index